CUBE ROOT OF BOOK

T0359810

Paul Magee was born in 1970 and grew up in
Melbourne. A scholar in classical languages,
Russian and the philosophy of history, he spent his
twenties between study, overseas travel, and work
as a freelance Latin tutor. The University of Illinois
Press published his prose study of travel, *From
Here to Tierra del Fuego*, in 2000. He is a lecturer in
creative reading at the University of Canberra.

CUBE ROOT OF BOOK

Paul Magee

JOHN LEONARD PRESS

ACKNOWLEDGEMENTS

Poems and sequences from this book have appeared in *Blast*, *Blue Dog*, *Cordite*, *Island*, *The Journal of the Classical Association of Victoria*, and *Salt-lick Quarterly*.

I am indebted to John Leonard, as editor, for helping these words to surface.

My Mum was always there too, my father, my sisters and brothers.

To Bertie.

First published 2006 by
John Leonard Press
PO Box 1083
Elwood, Victoria 3184, Australia

National Library of Australia
Cataloguing-in-Publication data:

Magee, Paul, 1970–.
Cube root of book.
ISBN 0 9775787 1 2
   1. Title.
   A821.3

Design: Sophie Gaur
Photo: Roberta Walker
Printed and bound by BPA Print Group, Burwood, Victoria

Set in Goudy

CONTENTS

Chapter 1 / 1

Chapter 2 / 5

Chapter 3 / 11

Chapter 4 / 15

Chapter 5 / 21

Chapter 6 / 27

Chapter 7 / 31

Chapter 8 / 37

Chapter 9 / 45

Chapter 10 / 51

Chapter 11 / 61

Chapter 1

1

But what else is left
to halt this falling
unprophesied night?

2

a shout

3

There's no Hell on earth
like that we give each other
for nothing have this poem

4

Total recall
the date the year
and other related things like
relationships
rings of age
for things that don't grow on trees
include happiness
cracked
like a glass framed photo
and sing along
with tomb swinging

I will tell you the whole truth, Trojan King, whatever may
become of it, he said, and I won't deny my Peloponnesian roots.
That's the first point. For even if Fate has left Sinon
a broken man, she shall not, with all her cruelty, make me practise
deceit. Perhaps some word got into your ears of Palamedes.
He was Belus's son, Palamedes, he was famous to the stars.
With a false charge of treason, a snake's allegation, and only
    because
he'd once opposed their war, the Greeks struck him down
for death; but now they mourn his absence from this light.
He was the man to whom my impoverished father sent me
from my earliest years, to act as his companion-in-arms against you
to come fight here. While reigning safely, he stood tall in
    committees
of the kings – as did I – earning their respect and our power.
But when Palamedes was struck by the envy of that two-face
    (believe me,
I know) Ulysses, and sank down from the world above
I drowned my days out, in broken spirits, in shadows, in grief
at the destruction of my innocent friend, but raging inside.
And mad as I was I could not hold it in; I swore
that if I ever returned to our Achaean homeland, at the first
opportunity, and in the midst of our victory, I would
avenge him; and so I targeted their hatred upon me.
From that moment, I date the beginning of my fall; Ulysses
now began to terrify me with accusations of the unspeakable.
He started to spread his lying tongues about me in the crowd,
laid traps for me, sowed teeth against me, plotted with skill
relentlessly and then, with Calchas the priest in his pay –
But why am I telling you this wretched and pointless tale?
Why stop time? If you think that Greeks are all the same
the sound of Sinon's name alone will suffice; execute him right now.
That's what Ulysses would want, the Greek leaders would even pay
to see me gone.

Virgil, Aeneid II

6

They hew us from sex, we're born, we survive
put out an eye, they transplant us, we survive
roots pushing their way through the soul into soil

Leaf-shading we provide our own shade
till cut down to tables and chairs, seeming
semblances of life, stay alive

even onto this paper, this white
this skin's sharp feeling wooden flesh
life sits on us, like ink.

7

to personify the head you need a face
feet to do legs and shanks toes

each door is a lock, each key a prison
friendship is terrifying because it's you utterly

I get up and dress to visit (grave, my friend)
no worse than a tree that grows, breaks, breathes

8

Some scissors, sticks and stones
make a house
it's a basket
they put love in
these fish swim from my fingers
from your toes
the miracle is that we ever thought it was finite

9

By force of its stare
face full-sail
to the journey of dead flowers
to Eskimo kisses

10

Smoking one final cigarette
for the morgue, for my sins
a pack of twenty
brighter than death
a bunch of twenty flowers
a bundle of twenty sunsets
an incandescent torchlight
twenty variants thereof
a burning in the furnace
my limbs in fire
I forget about death
I see that cigarette therapy
has acquainted your poetry
with the colour red
said the stethoscope doctor
Stop sucking on that syringe
give me your hand
put your tongue on the match
your motor skills seem fine
will I give up?

11

When to the sessions of sweet silent
sessions of sweet silent sessions
of sweet silent thought things past

Chapter 2

1   *metamorphoses of brain damage*

The man who mistook his wife for a truck
they had a similar stress gradient
she bore her load of life badly
he lacked all emotion; his frontal lobes
had worn away like a brain-shaped
eraser; he'd lost that pencil with which we write
out the chorus of everyone else's responses to life
and sing along. I can't love you anymore she wrote
to him while in hospital, ever grinning
it's like you're there and not there
I don't care, he told the camera of his accidentally caused
lack of empathy, and she cried
on camera, and no one lied

the doctor looked on kindly
the camera and film crew watched
and so did I – in whose shoes (dress,
fingers, accident, blank screen or eyes)?

2   *and another*

'Rate your sadness for me,' she said to the woman, who was
trussed in a plaster cocoon like a broken leg
sensors and receptacles suspended from her to the ceiling

('I want to make you sad,' said the scientist
in her white like-a-slightly-longer-dress lab coat
'and to measure your frontal lobes')

'About a six' came a voice
whose bruise was real, if practised
large eyes staring out of old fruit sockets at the screen above

her, her words hanging spiders of text, set pain
('I'm a monster. I hate myself,'
the depressive wrote, with her fingers

typing out her saddest thoughts, quote unquote)
then while she was looking back at her thoughts
they radiographed the sadness of her brain

'I'm sad that you're sad,' the scientist then said
in her wordlessly-white, paper-white lab coat
'but I'm glad that you were sad for us';

like a child, the monster woman was still
sad but pleased to be pleasing, a little
healed, you could feel the plaster wearing lighter

and the power of science

3

There in Russia they keep their herds shut in stables, you'll see
no grasses in the fields, no leaves on the trees appear.
But the land is mounds of snow, shapeless and deep
in cold, it rises as you walk all around you. It's always winter,
the North-west wind is always breathing in frost.
His horses from morning reaching for the far skies, the Sun
never succeeds in scattering the paling shadows; his car rushes
to bathe in the red mirror of ocean. Night the shadows revives.
Bridges of ice congeal, of a sudden, from flowing rivers. Whose
    waves
then carry wheels bound with iron on their backs. Having
once served ships, they now pave a way for open carts.
The cold causes bronze vessels to leap apart, clothing stiffens
when put on, they cut off blocks of frozen wine with an axe.
While pools, in their depths, turn solid ice, fierce icicles
make caves of uncombed beards, and the snow
all through the air, is all this time falling.

Virgil, Georgics III

4

Some God's elbow escarpment holds this town in to
its azure seascape, its fresh mown green back yards,
Hill's hoist, sea-saw waves and sky-blue time

a shivering pall over the death of our dead friend
whose loss we have gathered to forget, whose loss
to forget, bright eyes embrace me, you've arrived

5

Dean wanted a cigarette. I suggested
he watch *The Curse of the Phantom Limbs* instead:

They're interviewing a woman and her stump
which feels, which she feels, pain
in the fingers, though she lost it from the elbow

A hand typing in the distance, next door, on the computer

An artist interviews her too, takes photos, digital
images and then virtuals
the woman's imagined pain in, pixelling a massive swollen hand
(the hand that grasped the wheel – this is imprinting)
on a stick-thin arm attached to the stump: a map of pain
an artist paints

            *

Another is a man with no arm, but his phantom
body map has a huge thumb, a thumb for an arm

                        The typing stops
Dean didn't need a cigarette. He wrote a letter instead
touch-typed like us

6

A man lost all sensation in his right arm
from the motorcyke smash, but his phantom hand still gripped in
     pain.
The eyes. Their phantom pain. The arm ungripped
(its ghostly impossible grasp. What else are phantoms
but. And so is art. This is imprinting the scientist said print. The
homunculus in your brain is more you than you. Which remaps)
when he placed the one left in the black mirror box.
In a mirror your right arm is your left
a reflection of the left. So you see

both limbs, one virtual, one real, move perfectly now, as if the
     motorbicycle
had never cut the other off. And patients start to cry
And to lose all phantoms float away pain

     *

a cigarette
paints phantom lungs

7

The body of Bethesda: the tain of sky that floats overhead
and the walking tracks vein the land with life

inroads, humans, ring up in the mind
their binary codes, the lizard beside me, DNA-determined

he motes in the eye my *silence of nature*
as if the divorce I'm getting over meant as much to him

as the light at each tick of the clock of the sun
on the pool of Bethesda, silence settles, no one
was or ever will be at home

8

Walking around a
corpse makes
the path of our
conversation
difficult, trippy, little
jumps in grammar
excuse me

9

Can the plastic plastic surgeons

cut out ugly successes, make faceless

a clean canvas, skin smooth as paper

10

Cleaning my teeth with a truck

11

I ate the best minds of my generation rot dribbled
down the sides of my chin and not throwing up
To what sight
do you shut that eye off
do you dream it to death
do you drink it all down
to one black painting
that swallows the frame

Chapter 3

1

. . .only the testosterone
was somehow inhibited. She became herself, unaware
that she could never have children. Adoption had failed her
and her husband. She didn't quite explain why. But her features
being slightly more masculine were all the more feminine, her
 biology
teacher explained. The devastated seventeen-year-old girl
still to menstruate, now finding out why, broke down
and the teacher showed her, to calm her, the genes xy
in a sample of her blood, and repeated that masculine features
actually enhanced feminine beauty. Tall and striking, now forty-five
divorced. Her husband never knew that his teen love was
a man, not only on the inside, but all through till she told him.
For how can you hide from your truth, in a body, when it's not
even you? The marriage survived through trauma, and died.
The woman and her teacher were reunited after an ad-break

by the producers, and she cried, in her body, she cried
at her secret, to its first sharer, the human body, her teacher.

2

There are hundreds of homes
for us here in my mind
said one bee on the verge
of psychosis

3

Now I shall describe the gifts of air-born heavenly honey.
Attend to this portion too of my poem, Maecenas.
I shall sing of vistas to amaze you in the world
of little things, their great-minded leaders, their customs
and callings, their nations and battles, all in order;
my work treats of a slight theme, but the glory will be great
if the adverse powers allow it, if Apollo hear my prayer.
First one must find a place, a home for the bees
free of the wind's advances – for the wind forbids
food to be brought home. Do not allow sheep, or
little head-butting goats to trample down the flowers,
keep baby cows, wandering in the plains, from shaking
the dew free, or wearing away the grasses as they grow.
Keep the painted lizards with their stiffening spines
far from the rich houses, along with the bee-eaters
and the other birds, Procne the swallow among them
whose breasts bear the marks of her own bloody hands.
For they lay waste to all around. They fly off with bees
in their mouths, as sweet snacks for their merciless young.

Virgil, Georgics IV

4

I paint my nails icy blue
I drag on an outfit
I paint my eyes the rosy hue
of broken glass
off my dress you bitch
I'm you

5

Portrait of a portrait as a young portrait

6

Eyeliner
mirrors
the weather
a tear
photographs
concrete
keys
dead leaves
the four winds

7

These noises scraping as fingernails on blackboards all around me
a classroom this room my vase that sings in tune
out of tune in tune
no table
the stage is constituted by the shattering of a vase

8   *Sydney postcard*

that bleary-faced old faith of me supping on the sober
the podium dancers were podium dancing

and the night did away with all thought of the night
yet Icarus found it easy to sprawl into the Sun

did his skies slip from knowing
did the soles of his feet come undone

Hyde Park spreading out its dark rug of grass
to eternity

an eye enters the harbour smashes a mallet smashes down on a
face my hand touches his breast like the wheels of the train go
round and
                                    round

9

Mouth the hand that comes out of this mouth
by itself

a whole keyboard I spat
by someone else in myself

to play deaf with yourself
or to write with two ears

that's music (at my desk)
or to write with two hands

10

You're an actress
playing both parts
of Pelléas
and Mélisande

You're on the spot
and can not sing

There are no words
and you must kiss
on-stage
to an audience
of
your very self

11

Drink to me with broken eyes only and I'll not look

Chapter 4

1

My father died
three years to this day
or another like it

I could have jumped into the grave
like Ophelia's pond, like Hamlet

Frogs leap and play in the mud the rain

I had a coffee instead
with someone I hate

2

Son, I want you to have my
so cattle are branded
so one dreams of foreign lands
through these windows
one day we'll fly
and find you again
leaving the relics behind
and ahead and all in pieces

3

And the cursed father, no longer a father, said 'Icarus!
Icarus,' he said, 'where are you? Where am I to find you?
Icarus!' he kept saying, till eyeing the boy's wings in the waves.
Deploring his own creations, the father buried his son's body
in a mound on Icaria – that's how the island got its name. And
    while
Daedalus was placing the bones of his poor boy in the grave,
a chattering partridge looked on from a muddy ditch,
applauded with his wings, and in song testified
to his joy. Only recently transformed, he was the sole
bird of his race still, his fate an everlasting reproach
to you, o inventor. For Daedalus's sister, unaware
of how Fate would call, had apprenticed her son to him:
Partridge, a boy of twelve years, his mind open to learning. Already
he had cut rows of teeth in sharp steel, taking for his model
the backbone of a fish. Thus he discovered the saw. He had
bound with one knot two steel legs; one would stand fast
while the other, at a constant distance, would draw in
a circle. Daedalus, jealous of his nephew, threw him
from the holy citadel of Athens. 'Partridge fell,' he lied.
But the boy, whom Athena adored for his mind,
was caught by the goddess and returned as a bird:
feathers formed in mid-air, the force of his mind,
already birdlike, slipped into feet and wings, his name
alone remained. Not quite. For the partridge, despite his wings,
does not trust himself to heights, nor lodge his nests
on the tips of tall branches. Near the ground he flies,
lays eggs in hedges and, ever a memory of his ancient fall,
fears heights.

Ovid, Metamorphoses VIII

4
snakes
because we don't have hands
to control
over anything
not even our language

rivers
which are the same
as serpents sinuously
shifting surfaces over time
and land, and sky

the rainbow
and its refractions
is the subject
of a scientific treatise by Spinoza
these words too

5
I lay down my loss by the Elwood canal

whose memory is long
whose lines run to ripples
whose tide is all time

I lost my father here, or somewhere like it
he had words for all weathers
he had time for low tides

The moon reflects on my loss, this dark night

6

    Photos take on words and speak
for the dead who took them. He left me
    a camera, single lens
reflex colour film inside, that I
    remembered, three years later
to open and bring to light. The next
    day returned twenty-four prints
in a surreally damaged pink light
    stained as if sun set and I
cried, when I saw none of him. Thus he
    had documented, for
insurance purposes, the last house
    in which we lived, twenty-four
photos, light-damaged, of a Perth house
    that wasn't home enough to –
setting chemicals images things so
    cruelly; then I felt my eyes
hold him in its frame: *You are my house.*

7

An average suburban sowing among fields of houses,
cars, concrete, occasional trees, eyes sewn up, gently
unsewn once more, cyclically, on the road past sorrow

But how high is the city of Melbourne?
the tallest building?
and if I lose the law of gravity, going up

just when will I stop living here
The sky begins at our toes

but words presume that you won't disappear
how do you die?

8

The orchestra, dressed the colour of night
floating on black water

immersed into a wall on the back of my throat
in Novosibirsk on the twenty-third of August 2002

Hold it to your chest, your absence
invoke it at all moments

a life-saving cavity
an instrument around it resounding

when life is missing
and he comes running through your chest

his eyes, your aorta-broken heart
(giving up reading, listening to music,

playing)
he becomes your death. Now sing

9

The dispute between Summer and Autumn
entailed much suffering

The heat burst back with ripe fruits
twigs hardened and pointed

A brilliant day seemed
to fall too soon

Like Autumn it will pass
as leaves rustle, old papers
drift past, pass us by

10

(Here
optic nerves
dangle
they are open poppies
in the evening
air)

I must have blinked

Teach me the meaning
of the simplest words
without using an
example

11

Telescope the dark heavens in
to a dark star, five hundred watts,
eye-light burning

A tongue plummets to this Earth of death the rock of Lazarus.
Swelled in his
throat it speaks

All this time melted over morning
tea and
my dead

Row boat no it won't
like silence oars words
You

Chapter 5

Few botanists are fluent in both Chinese and English
which is why some of the plants are not fully identified
in the South China garden, though the *paeonia suffruticosa*
first grown in imperial gardens, are known and named
for their showy flowers. A national passion, they bloomed
from 700 AD at the Festival of Ten Thousand Flowers, perhaps
    rivalling
oroxylum indicum, One Thousand Papery Seeds, whose pods
grow to one metre long, in ostentation and display
while the seeds (each pod contains thousands) would
become fans for emperors, for the wealthy, for the memory
of you that now unfurls as I chance upon this winter
garden soon to become spring (as will the Californian garden,
the rainforest, the basil plantings, the Chinese windmill palm
used to make coats).
           You need the warmth
of the untranslated to survive the world. That tree
there has no name, it just grows, like a day we chase
to keep up, it's a tombstone – contrary to appearance
tombstones are never inscribed, words fail us
we just pretend to have names

2

Merri Creek is she happy, washed-up, plastic?
The aftertaste exists it's real
It was some other bridge
mirrors, daily

Put a knife
through the eye
of the Sun
with a twist that says
you're not real
but your death
the real recyclable
floating garbage

that you could build a house on
and swing from the rafters
like a creek-jumping child
with bottle-top treasures for eyes

3

You're distant
in the distance

or up close
next to me

Your eyes are worlds
as this Earth
is an ocean

You glance away
to watch the sea

4

So many, over so many lands, through so many bodies of water,
I've travelled, my poor brother, to attend your funeral
and present you with the final gifts you'll receive. I've come
to speak to your voiceless ashes in vain, now that chance
has snatched you from me, o my brother, o poor brother,
so unjustly torn from me. In the meantime, but that's all there
    can be
and by the beautiful custom of our forefathers, accept what
was given to the dead: these lonely funeral gifts of wine, milk
honey and words, they're dripping with a brother's tears.
And for all the future, my poor brother, fare well, but you've gone.

Catullus, Carmen CI

5

A bleak question mark
(suddenly shifts
in response
to your reading
takes on tone
colour
complexion
sunrises
confusion
then
semantically
sunsets)
Time grows
in circles
by the hour
as a suicide
or stone in water
sets off rings of
phone call rings
in circles

6

                                              how I
the town crier, proclaim grief

how every table I set it on, disappeared

how people die now and then, they're no support

nor are trees, nor even leaves, the bare books just outside
how do you bring a dead person up to life?
with your teeth you eat

7

My body was racked by demons for a long time
they stretch you by the fingers
ever so slightly as you're writing
forking love on your soul
sharpening up the pencils in your eyes

entertaining suicide an
instant stage, bright lights, train smack through you
that threw you into this traffic with life

and I realise as I'm writing this that I'm rewriting
my sister's suicide note that she never left

8

Chick peas are older than beans, than trees with
edible leaves, than all other domesticated crops.
Hummus tastes back to the first farmers, chance discovered
I suppose – it's before history – you eat it
with a paprika garnish and a sprig of green leaf,
something modern like parsley, a tablespoon of olive oil
and all of human life; it's just a symbol, a story,
tombstone teeth, and the memory of breathing
the last thing to die, is to die

9

You suicided all my poetry was written on your skin first
line
second line
third line a tight rope tight knife

At the private hospital they hid their ailments
from each other
bedside tables
bursting with tears

The hospital library is little
but the books expand beyond the shelves
drowning lips kiss through the page
and open worlds in your palm

I walked in to the locksmith
who speaks Russian to me: как ты поживаешь?
I'm fine, thanks
I was unlocked

by the memory
of the teeth
of the lock
I became when

my hand drawing close
was released from its scream
faced into the day
I opened doors your death lightly

10

And her hands are kneading our love
a doughy bankruptcy that smiles
lumps of love in the face mixed up
she hurls us like clay malformed

My eyes went missing in action
my sister
talked computers, possession, dogware, love, commitment

only to be told that if she was well enough to commit herself,
she was well enough to look after herself. Beds were needed for
the involuntary cases. Perhaps for cases like herself, involuntarily
committed so often in the past

and I all of thirteen handed her to the police
I'd like it all back
Have you ever betrayed someone?

Once, after I had spent hours convincing her just to stay in
the same room with me, to put the scissors down, that the dog
hadn't been programmed by our parents to spy on us, that I
wasn't squeezed up against the wall like an eggwhite eyeball,
that the television was our friend, that the police now arriving
weren't the police, Bridget knowing full well by now that I
had been deceiving her, that I was handing her over to them
– that's called commitment – stopped on the threshold of the
room from which she was now being led, the prospect of yet
more months in the sick heavens of psychotropic drug stupor
ahead of her. On the threshold she looked back. I was a mess
in a chair, my face in my hands. 'I love you, Paul,' she called
back to me, like the ghost she now is, 'Do you love me?' And I,
like the ghost I am, couldn't answer.

Chapter 6

1

Mia unclasps her new umbrella
its pictures of people, shopping people
Pokémon sort of people, presses
the button and shoots the rain
red little umbrella, rain-shooting
and takes on the skies, cloudstorming
rainbursting, shopping people para-
chuting from the sky, little people
flying all around us the rain

2

A pastoral poem
with a table outside
made of trees
a carpet of grass
the dead are alive
picking flowers
in every letter we write
ho little sheep, passing by
and smiling bees

3
Your bookcase is a hideaway for angels
who sidle nightly in between novels
and stories, poems and science, to sleep
two-dimensionally, as pressed flowers
by night, but as angels, who are abstract and quiet

4
This poem is

(true
or false)

5
The clouds are all knots inside
a Klein bottle sunset
on this strangely topological
day now night
the universe expands, it's a torus

(a clay coffee cup with a handle may be
– they are topologically equivalent –
smoothly transformed into a doughnut)

or a universe, to a kid at McDonalds

6
Imagine reading this
poem in braille, even the
words that don't count you feel

7

I hate the public, I push it away

(Observe this poem in
ritual
silence, I am its priest).

Songs never before sung
I bring to the ears
of our delicate young

men and women. Jupiter
(kings have dominion
over their sheep, but He

over kings lords it, is famed
for the Giants' defeat)
with a wink shifts all life.

                                  Horace, Odes III

8

Who cut my ears off?
Love wonders
a lily flower playing in his blood

The lily
knows that silence
is a poem about nothing

She's free as this breeze
she's in Love, pools
of Love

9

Summer flowed backward
one year into spring
and that was fine, so fine
to see flowers grow
younger, unwrinkle, grow
greener, disappear

Love's frozen over
in fear of an answer
to the question
on its chafed lips:
what will Autumn
backward bring?

10

The stars are not seen
by day but there they are
let the heavens burst through
this blackest of days

11

Shall I compare thee to a Shakespearean sonnet?
The rain forms beads on a cosmetic cheek.
Dark of day, what season is raging outside?
Helen Keller understood
lightning
from the way ideas strike
a match
(with a metaphor)

Chapter 7

1   *Lucia di Maribyrnong*

Father let me leave this house
sings/sighs the daughter from her fortress
her eyes on the workman here to fence her in.

Audience bored, chatter, twitter, fat man sleeps
The opera's not begun till the fat man sleeps to the end.
Prima donna glares, dagger in hand, assumes the stage.

Second act – the tenor grieves his mother –
Third act – the daughter kills her husband –
Ohime!, Orrore! – on the night of their wedding

this vow-breaking wedding, a rent in the fabric
of heaven, the curtains all falling around,
breast-beating and screaming out tears, as

six voices in synchrony
six reactions to the scene
six lines take to the ceiling
a geometry of passion
a pin-point

2   *Mr Ruddock's speechwriter (Philippic I)*

The asylum in a desert swallows the phrase, a throat
a drain with birds circling, a gate

it's hard to think you're alive when there's nothing but blank
pages inside the pick lock of these eyes cut

poor man, didn't *conceive* those children nine months
in the public mouth, hanging off his nipples, his nose

I mass produce myself in a moment
I stamp me through myself.

That took a while,
to hold it in – that, on the shelf

is my speech
it tried to fly away, so I learned it

(and you're the same)
gulp

    *   *prayer*

A poem he never wrote reads to itself the lines on her face
the woman who returned from the ocean which sank her husband
please, let them take some words as they go (lover, child)
don't die without saying our names (brother, friend, sister, another
        friend)
for ever – it's just a moment to God
please, let them take some words as they go
for ever – it's just a moment

3

The nightmare at hand is anaesthetised, but so is blood.
The initial letter of a medieval page paints a scribe:

iconic knife of trade in the left, and quill sharpened
to pick up dragonsblood in the right

hand (you mix it in to the sap of any shrub).
A jar contains brazilwood, for which red-ink-

bearing-trees the nation was named, far in the future
when books were already the crops of paper

unlike Folio 27695h,
in the British Library, which once had eyes and ate.

Once the skin of sheep
or calf, also pig, squirrel and hare, even deer

was stripped from the animal and washed in clear
cold running water one day and night, and began to rot,

the hair fell out and their
skins were scraped to parchment on a beam,

heads cut off, and then hides folded
from A3 to B4, always rectangular, because so

was its exemplar
– shorn of legs – and we

still today read books with rectangular pages.
Only we illustrate the letters in our sleep.

4   *for a prime minister (Philippic II)*

and the case now being tried
is one of suicide who did it
who killed you from inside
your own throat
they laid carpet over the depression
and walled the walls with love
s-bend dweller
s for suck harder
I feel you uptight, a succession
of dying deaths, of days
when your face falls in
you do all you can
to hold up your eyes, your nose, your skin.

5

Depression
means you're on the edge
of a pleasure
you don't want
to surrender because
it will kill you
sing the dishes
as I wash them clean

6

There's more dead people in this world
than living
for the dead once dead stay dead
for the living once dead disappear

7

You play out death

in every breath

you take
but where

are you taking them from

is a logical proposition
followed by a question
that's a question

for someone
deader than I

8

Don't even try to ask your Gods – it's not ours to know –
what bounds they've set upon us, Leuconoe. Also:
get rid of your Babylon horoscopes. Whatever happens
things are better that way. And know this.
Whether Jupiter has many more winters in our jar
or if the Adriatic squall now breaking on the soft
volcanic rocks of this shore breathes our last – let the wine
breathe, cut your hopes to moments.
Since I wrote this, Envy and Time have shrunk away.
Rip today from the paper. Don't ever trust what's yet to come.

Horace, Odes I

9

A big pond in a small fish
Look on my works, ye miserable, and repair

J. Kennett, politician (Philippic III)

10

Two men, their compelling flesh, close-pressed and driving
hard. And the fascist Judge kisses, fucks and is fucked
by the oldest of the boys, in all the equality of lust now a man,
on top, perhaps in love, and certainly desiring
to pleasure the source of law by coming inside it: in *Salo*.
For *Salo* is a work of freedom and love: a repressed dream.

A voice off-screen lovingly recites *Canto IXC* over the
following and final scene while the Judge, outside now, and in day
proceeds to cut out the eyeballs of his victims, to drip blood on
their alabaster flesh slowly, and not block his ears
to their extreme cries of pain beyond the reach of mercy,
staining each line of Pound's text with dream as memory
sees through the poem, the torture, the dark night fuck
in the previous scene, as children die, as credits roll.

11

What would happen if you breathed?
a hidden lung a word swallowed
a bird in the throat got your tongue
for one of its young
a look of divorce in your eyes

Chapter 8

I

From steel sheet faces
he made up conversations
of high stress grading

and nuts and bolts
for tears in his eyes

then he
cut another corner
sharp

in the deduction process. We don't
at this factory, make friends to last

you have to bolt your face in to love
and that will save you spare parts. There's just

one for a man, to fall apart

when you come close
to his body
and you wonder
is it me
on the other side
of that flesh?

2

I don't mind the hospital inside my head
it operates on its own
passengers
a double decker bus
on the operating table, exhaust
pipes, eardrums, gearsticks
the tiniest bones in the body
steering wheels of the mind
a bus crash recurring
mathematically recurring
go into the accident
trace your features
chalk lines around an arm
a leg over there, life lines
turning skies into weather reports
roads into stop signs
people into handshakes
looks in the eye.

There are lots of things to think through
your brain for one
Think through death
and you're already dead
this tapestry
sewn up eyes, staked moments, no time.

3

'Dear nurse, fetch my sister Anna, tell her
to sprinkle her body with river water, she must hurry
to bring the animals with her, the other offerings, we will
sacrifice them as prescribed. Have her come to
the pyre, and take a sacred ribbon to cover your brow.
I intend to conclude the holy rites, already prepared
as prescribed and begun, to Jupiter of the Underworld,

to put an end to my cares, to hurl an effigy
of Aeneas's head into the flames, and atone,' Dido said.
With an old woman's eagerness, the nurse hastened along.

*

A shout went up to the high halls. The rumour ran
like a madman through the close-shocked city, the ceilings
of buildings rumbled with weeping, with groaning
and the wails of women, the upper air echoed with grief.
It was as if all Carthage, or ancient Tyre, had been destroyed,
the enemy was within and passionate flames twisted
through the houses of men, the houses of the Gods.
She heard: out of her mind, terrified by the incessant running,
ripping her face with her nails, hitting her chest to make it real,
Dido's sister rushed through the crowd, and called upon her
dying sister by name: 'Was this why? Just to deceive me?
The burning, the altars, the flames – just for this? How am I
even to begin to blame you, now that you've left me alone?
Why didn't you ask me to come too? Out of pride?
You should have asked me to share with you. Both of us
could have suffered the same hour the same cut in the heart.
Instead you had me build your death-bed, with my own hands
you had me invoke our ancient Gods, with my own voice
so that you could lie here and do away with yourself. Slaughterer!
You've killed yourself, you've killed me, you've killed the people
and statesmen of Carthage, you've wiped out your own city.
Sister, let me wash your dying wounds with water
if you still breathe up here above, let me catch your last
breath, as it falls from your lips.'

*

The Trojan hero, pausing nearby, recognised the dim form
of Dido the Phoenician, her wound still weeping, as
she wandered among the shades and shadows of the great forest
just like the crescent moon, which one sees,
or thinks one sees, through the clouds. Recognising her
he suddenly cried tears, and called out to his sweet, lost love:
'O poor Dido, so it was true, the report that you had ripped
your final moments from a sword. Because of me you died?
By the stars, by those above, if there is any faith
to be held here in the depths of the earth, by that also
I swear, Dido, I left Carthage against my will.
The Gods ordered me. The Gods who now compel
me to pass through these cloud-drawn and decaying
derelict zones, this depth of night where you live –
they drove me with their commands. How was I to know
that my leaving would bring such suffering back
to you? Stop. Don't leave my eyes. Who are
you fleeing? This is the last thing I am ever fated to say
to you.' With words like these, Aeneas attempted to placate
her spirit of its pure fury, to soothe its feral glare
and, himself crying, sought to rouse her to tears.
She held her eyes fixed on a point far away from his.
Her face was no more moved by the speech he had begun than
a hard flint stone, or a mountain on the isle of Paros. Finally –
hating him intimately and forever – she tore herself away
and fled to the shaded hollow in the woods, where her former
husband Sychaeus answers to her woes, where love is requited.
Stricken by the Hell of it, Aeneas followed her there
with his tears, lamented her loss again, and felt pity.

Virgil, Aeneid IV & VI

4

It was not my day to begin with:
your funeral, brilliant smog-blue day
by the beach, my cigarette on top of the flu
a blast of chill air through the church
another self-killing and the underside
of every word is anger, resentment, laughter
strange lust – they really loved him – football scarf
wrapped around the cold comfort coffin
and the memory of his goodness I'd forgotten
rips a hole in the throat of this apple-bitten day
that was not mine to begin with, thank God

5

and walls of words to wall in
the first person pronoun
forthwith declared to be
null and void in sense
herein sentenced to
the involuntary care
of the missing Department
of Missing Persons State
of Collapse *Amen*

6

We're always facing forward, I realised reading Blake
forward that our heads don't know inward
eyes or nose his Jerusalem. We turn
to look, still outside. That city of one
dives its full height inside.

7

Postmarked
and the writing on the back

Buildings arising
pin-cushion like
out of the night
how many angels
fit on top of this
building arising
pin-cushion like
out of the night

Crash test dummies
must feel this way
at the moment of impact
before the moment of impact
at the moment of impact
before the moment of impact

I'm a postcard collector
my favourite is an odd view
of Sydney by night
my throat flies through my chest
no it hasn't happened yet
my lungs stick to my back
no it hasn't happened yet
my legs shatter into ankles
no it hasn't happened yet

8

This is mine now
roses burst into flame
from my finger tips
glances melt into wax
into fire

a
boundless
infinite ink

My hold on this world is tenuous
at the best of times, this is one
hand but what are hands for
so tenuous?

That hand sculpture before me
real and cubist and surreal – that
passing stranger passing

9

Down forty floors
of fathoms
Front cover
title page
preface
introduction
contents
index
the end
is just beginning

to hurt
The book
of one hundred and one
suicides
begins slowly
pages one to five
new ways of dying
and then speeds up
page eighteen
haiku
car crashes
at thirty

10

The path of least renaissance

11

When you read you don't see
what you read, nor it you.
But seated again: the head, the feet
the eons between
use the chair for their back.

Chapter 9

1

In that country
manna grew on trees
the stems of flowers
were straws to
pools of ambrosia underground
it rained upward
and the tendency when you leapt
was to lose yourself in the stars
through flying fish
flying by
The horizons harbour oceans
of horizons
and wake next to you

2

I cut in half Proust's remembrance of
because it kept falling on my falling asleep
head
like a dream (all remembering)
of a strange book to cut in half waking
up
to myself cut in half by
things past

3

I feel the unease of it touching the sides
of your throat only words
and I wanted only to scream

little baby versions of me
in you
in me

4

All at sea, I held you
for three hours of psychotic
squaller, her voices in my head
my only friend, do you love me?

'You wallpapered my mind with floral kisses
with space for windows, posters, a picture, garden
view – why was I not happy?'

5

I love you my evening
my darling, my daily disappearance, my surrender
all alone, my black sun, my life giving night
you give loss a wanton guise, till morning

6   *quartet*

punching the speaker in
and the phone my tongue a soldering iron
leaking ingots of hate
to the receiver, receive her love slam
down hate of the phone

*

the floor of the car for gears, accelerate
out of street left right smile at strangers
I don't live here I'm just eating air
the bridge bulwark ploughs like an iron through the water
stands still and blurs in the silent river
flows in creases, river, car crash and debris,
passers by, words as I watch
without heads and into the night

joggers jog in and out like ramrods

myself a broken bottle of a face

houseminding every word you say

*

opening I entered was within
no space no face to
contort into a smile for
and dark and damp as the city
I grew up one day in Melbourne
hatched a bird's nest of children from
my mouth squealing and crying for their
love like little birds, and singing
it's not so bad

*

dutiful daughters at the laundromat
washing the gods from their sheets
by the rivers of idle nights, pools
bells, desert heat, sighs
to rouse fathers from their graves
to sleep
by her side as the sand

7

You ask, my Lesbia, how many
of your kissing kisses, how many
would more than satisfy me? As many
as grains of Libyan desert spread
from horny Jove's sun-stoned oracle
in silphium-rich Cyrene to
the holy tomb of ancient Battus;
when night puts human loves on view
as many as guilty stars collude,
to kiss you – that many kisses
would more than satisfy Catullus
for-all-the-Earth insane, and then
the prying could not add them up
nor envious mouths them all consume.

Catullus, Carmen VII

8

We are as different
as darkness and light
when they touch

You said, yours
in darkness and light
I said, teach me to hold on
I'll teach you to let go
but hold me all the same

9

You wanted me to be as absolute
as pavement as steel-jawed as the sun
but even concrete setting looks like
the waves above us tumbling
even buildings crash when you
                    jump

hop-scotch, with one foot in front of
the other, the clouds wrong way
death and dying is always success
                    full
                    the end

but the mind is as stable as a horse that bolts

you jump
your body follows
it lands
you land too

My love, my gentle Sufi
you were spinning on the spot
with bracelets on your ankles
and leaping in your eyes
into bed, in your mind, when I said
shall we kiss?
This page now
bears the imprint of your body
ruffled sheets, rounded shadow

Were our words too perfect?
did they leave you no shadow?

e.g.
egg
i.e.
I eat
n.b.
nibble
p.s.
parsley
word-salad
etc.
electro-cetera shock of eating my own words once more in love

                                                              that
                                                           sudden
                                                           asylum

Chapter 10

1

I didn't make Siberia, the thought of queues Russia-wide
for tickets, to do anything in Russia is like eating this book –

*

the memory, though, I'd restore, like an old icon, of Yakutsk
where the Lena's seamless mirror of self-reflecting sky
accompanied me for three night-days of partying on a cruise boat
with the local Soviet dee-jays and I slept with a woman
whose child had died there. Every second year she'd return
to lay flowers, and I, only twenty, didn't understand
death or what it meant, not to have a child. Her father had been
a diplomat, her accent thick and seventies
bespoke an American youth, though life there was
arrested. A curtain on her mother's *misconstructions*; who'd
failed to stop the words migrating from her mouth
We were together one night. I guess I was her stranger.

*

Chinese restaurant, Yakutsk, bar-room fight.
People sway like drunk drumsticks impossibly upright.
Eat your postcards and photos, sing along.

Two days back and already the glare of the cold broke my back
in Melbourne, at the laundromat, I hate travel
that turns into here. Stop. In Moscow, at the Mayakovsky
Museum, my Russian flooded back, at an eyeball keyhole
stare into the flat where he shot through. To speak.
I'd forgotten how, after twelve years of absence. Each floor is a
different colour, red for blood, revolution, the wringer of gnats,
Stalin, Mayakovsky's official fan. Yellow for fear,
and collages of bits of paper and glass: documents, books,
the debris of a life washed up. But how and what is this metaphor,
drying out now in the machine: the me it's been
these last three months of travel comes to a rest in creases, to
lie crumpled, to feel the warmth of steel machine on its shoulders.
Breathe me back. Speak:
The Pushkin Institute of Russian Language and Literature is still
     communist
in appearance: liquid paper grey white walls, mistakes
of architecture, taste or indifference, rise from Ulitsa Volgina
to grace the skies with their absence from the memories of anyone
but me. I lived here ten mad months (a gestation plus one)
as *perestroika* collapsed all around me and my mind
a Soviet mess of rancid porridge, chipped brick-work and learning
(you learn to count bricks, to grow up, to lose a job, to feel walls)
while I, all of twenty, discovered depression and mania,
they're the same, in Russia, for the first time, among a people
who believed, by its very absence, in a soul; and drank vodka,
the drink of old believers. Today
I stepped out of the metro where it broke down
at Sportivnaya, and then flew to my old home on the outermost
     ring
of Moscow's Yuri Gagarin orbit of satellite suburbs; glory
to the cosmonaut, to the workers, to earthly stars, planets of love
gone kitsch, the outer space within us all: the Pushkin
no one's home

3   *Californian wedding*

So that bed of a book I carried travelling one week
cost fifty bucks, and then over the course of the wedding
as I struggled to read every word that wasn't
just authority, I found myself sleeping, slower
than her slow prose. Burning books in dreams
I committed her words to the flames; waking up
I opened the grate,
Poetry and the Fate of the Senses met its fate:
through 450 pages: footnotes, slowly dribbling
centipedes of speech from the mouth.
Then next day, skin still dreaming, scuba-diving
alongside the pipes that once brought fish
by pump from offshore boats to Cannery Row,
just as Steinbeck flooded words on the page:
we're all oceans

   *

and you, my passing love, found orchid
shapes in words, in schools of fish, in the fragile
folds of pink on your wedding dress visitor's breast
and I, a guest like you, fell in love, or the sea
or the flames of folds of the ocean's embraces:
the fate of the senses is to always stay alive
and occasionally to come up for air: Marry me!

UM, *Unaccompanied Minor*, a little girl of six, Katrina, Katryona
with a passport for Lietuva round her neck sat in front
of me on the plane, began to play with a doll, or with air.
'Hey little one,' I said, leaning over, 'this is how the radio works'

and headphone-headed she tried to listen to the kids' channel
in Finnish. Helsinki to Chicago, where little people land, the flight
of language through space is like words: can you catch them?
'My mom's in Chicago and my Dad pays money into a monthly

account.' She doesn't see him. I knew a word or two (three)
of Lithuanian: '*Labos ritos*' (Good morning). She replied 'But it's night.'
'Yes I know, but I – have you ever seen a kangaroo?' The flight
    attendant
wanted Katrina to eat her airline food. 'I only eat chocolate!'

and she did. Refusing to *behave*, which is the thing
all adults need you to be, or the plane will just crash into thin air,
a weird adult fear, as all six-year-olds know. We became friends.
'Tell her' (a little Lithuanian girl she'd found on the plane),

she demanded indignantly of me, and pointing,
that 'you're not my father.' I did, and Katryona translated
into Lithuanian, sure proof for her barbie-hugging buddy. 'I hate it,'
she said to me, 'when people think that someone is my father.'

And I *what's a father?* asked my mind, while the stewards flustered,
    all at sea
a six-year-old, UM, running around their knees, eating chocolate
making them look nervous. The six-year-old (international) solo
    traveller
settled on my lap, declined to eat salad with me, pulled my ears

as we read Lithuanian barbie doll magazines and discussed the
    nature of nature:
'There's people down there, right?' confirmed Katrina,
pointing to the ground, 'and no one lives up there?' (a gesture to the
    sky).
'So that means there are towns, without any people. Right?'

'Ye. . .yes,' I replied, and Chicago arose before my eyes
where I lived, at age six, first learned to fly, and that words
held us up; when my father suddenly died. Much, much later.
'Iki' in Lithuanian (Hello/Goodbye). For there are towns everywhere.

5   *Anna Karenina*

giving up
offerings to odd glances, through windows
of passing carriages of trains; and Gods
leap in front of us
in flames

the day depressed
for a smile somewhere got away
space dies with every suicide, and that's their gift
an empty emptiness

6

Then the sky turned on its point, and night fell upon Ocean,
covering Heaven, Earth and all the deceit of the Greeks
in its huge shadow. The Trojans, splayed out along the high
walls of the city, fell silent. Sleep embraced their weary limbs
in its arms, and I looked up the word for *patefactus*.

Virgil, Aeneid II

Anna H. Semyonoff also edited *The Captain's Daughter*. Her *New Russian Grammar*, in two parts, Edinburgh, 1934, ends in pain:

APPENDIX: verbs: *to put, to put hanging* i.e. *to hang*
is вешать, *to put oneself in such a position* is вешаться.
But вешаться *to commit suicide* does not belong to this group.
These verbs are not very common, especially вешаться, they were
not given in previous editions, examples follow:
He always hangs his coat in the wardrobe.
Today he put it on a peg in the hall (the train from Helsinki
to Petersburg translates me, my grammar reminds itself
of death). *She hangs on everyone's neck* i.e. gives
herself up. More often this is used as a perfective
verb: *Winter has come and hangs on tufts on the branches* (out the
window) *Pearls of rain are hanging* (a mini-death).
The past perfect in Russian becomes an English present tense:
Falling off the third floor, he hangs caught on a tree.
From the same root is
curtain, занавес (an Edinburgh curtain
on whatever's past or to come
I stare at Petersburg approaching
The train wheels leave it all behind)

*   *a painting in the Tretyakov, Moscow, 19th century*
Conscience is enshrouded in a metallic blue black
and a figure, drawing his dark shawl in tight
but featureless, is seen from the back, his eyes
on that distant corner of frame, where the betrayal
glows golden like a fire: it's Judas, who deliberates
on whether to black back into the foreground
of night. Among us. In treasures framed.

*

Peter the Great's Kunstkammer was begun in 1701
or in Hell, the crowds that gather are timeless:
an assemblage of freaks, double-heads, mermaid-
shaped foetuses with tail for legs, a Siamese twin,
a calf with five feet. Families of kids laugh and point
at each other. The exhibit was intended to medicalise
freaks of nature, to show that science, looking back in
through Petersburg's 'window on Europe,' could cast
(*mehr licht*) more light on things previously ascribed by and to
the Devil. Tongues. My guide, an Italian translation
like Petersburg itself, ushers us into the museum's
(*meravigliosamente kitsch*)
marvellously kitsch display of primitive culture,
displays it in double, but –
(*ciò che attrae i visitatori è in realta*)
what really attracts the visitor
are the freaks in the Kunstkammer;
(*è un divertimento*) it's a diversion
my lonely, lonely planet continues, *per tutta
la famiglia* and at this point I realise why I'm here
and hold back tears

from the window of light, because desire
is interpretation
of foreign language.
We're inside and bursting with bodies.
This room of speech.

8   *the restoration process*

The war in Grozny left paintings in pieces,
a museum by shells shattered, a broken shore
to an ocean of soul, or blood, art, peace.

The Tretyakov gallery in Moscow houses
(I remember once when the roof of our house
fell in. The chimney, blown down in a gale,
collapsed into the room I'd just passed
through, leaving a pile of dust, rubble, rain
reminding with each brick that the roof falls in
sometimes) icons of Russian art, national treasures,
the paintings which held a nation's breath
for seventy-five years, and now respiring
with before and after canvases
one a Christ
to show the restoration process,
the gallery is exhibiting paintings saved from Grozny
which burns with fire; God save us.
Paintings scored with lines, torn in part, shattered
and revived, look out and assert that art should be itself
a restoration – I was thirteen at the time and never knew
how that moment of collapse would come to paint
its way into all my later lives from marriage to death
a picture chases us – to tide us over all that gapes in the heart

and pictures are at best dressed wounds.
Our house came down long ago
and then you died.

Trying to decide, by the colours he chose, whether Matisse was
    happy
or sad, you realise that Picasso was neither. The paintings here
do my head in, each canvas cuts us up like life. A portrait.
At age twenty I loved this place, returned, as if to childhood,
again and again, to walk through Medieval doorways, on
    Michelangelo's *David*,
these full Parthenon friezes, all copies, in plaster cast to teach
the masses the pre-revolutionary meaning of cubism, of art. Copy.

The Matisse and Picasso are real: and insofar, are also copies
as is this day, who gave it? The deaths that have died since then
haunt all spaces, repeat me daily, cut up, like light through the
    window
carves a room in two, and sets the scene
for the gallery of copies you see daily.
At the Bolshoi Theatre
where orchestras, by the shape of their sounds
teach one to love paintings, I fear for my frame: Revolution!

10   *automatic teller machine*

                                        A night of sudden love
her laugh, and tottering drunk, we recited Pushkin's poems of love
right into each other's goodbyes, walking arm in arm.
The next day, two police by my side, happy to have found
me unregistered and ready for bribes, or a 'visit' to the station:
документи пожалуйства!
Only I pretended not to speak Russian to at least fuck up
part of their day, dawdled as they took me in, forced them
to wait as I, ballerina-like, paused to buy an ice-cream,
all the time harassing them in English till they found a tourist tout,
a seller of paintings – his father's, he told me, while translating a
fishy law, fifty dollars in bribes, and it's better, I think, for you
if you just pay.

Faces relaxed as the catch, giving in
obliged with a promise to bribe some justice back into things
via the ATM. A nineteen year old student
of finance and business, the tout walked me as if in chains.
'Do you paint?' I asked, if only to change pace. And he
getting chatty replied 'How do you like Russia?' and I
'I love it here!' automatically, while the policemen trailed
. . .It's just law and order, why not love it here? I thought.

Like his father, his children he told me
he hoped would be painters: 'How it goes,
one generation out and one in. I study finance
but my children will be artists.' You're a crook I thought,
an organiser of bribes, a daily sting, and that – stealing –
isn't far from speaking as an artist. At the ATM
I replied, 'Tell him, I'm a poet.' So he did.
Он поет – он говорит что поет.
Why the fuck do I need to know that?
The policeman looked pained, or like a stuffed pin, surprised
and said, with a look of swallowing incomprehension, 'Why?'

I don't know
but it had something to do with her eyes
and this poem, that I stole for her

II

words
any in particular?
yes

Chapter 11

I

It's as cold
as it gets in the tropics
(you carry your seasons inside)
I unpack, on the bus to Waikiki, my baggage-laden brain
after three months of throwing away
memories

Except her photos
they're in the mail, travelling behind me like the Chinese
soul I was told of in Moscow: you set out
on a trip and your soul arrives
a day or two later, it's a package, an image
an opening like the photos she took on that day from elsewhere

volcano-like the flows of tropical tongues of fern
a canopy of shade beside
a hot pond, her hair dripping Chinese black, floral eyes –
three months away, I remember nothing
a successful attempt to lose my mind
opening the photos she said she'd send in the mail

2

The last time I wanted time to end
I fell in love with you instead
like a boat tipping over the edge
of itself, I was floating
right-way up, swift sailing so fast
that the race of your desire
sailing away from me (with
you) walked around the corner
shall I ever see
hold your
keep

3

A three week long kiss
my eyes shut and
the roof the clouds
the ceiling the skies

as if meditating
with my lips
on your lips

with your lips
on my lips

I stole a kiss

4

Why does the day turn to glass and to bits us while
I from the corner
of the room
boxed
in like wallpaper
attempting
square patterns
to smile
out the gloss surface
the argument off our skin.
In a family photo.
(Our love's strung out on distant planets like drying negatives
we're fighting and I'm
just not here)
The pain in painting is flesh gouged
inches deep
go and pain an inch deep
canvas
unframe the words behind faces
speak
to me of love

5

The third person doesn't exist
he's she's your shadow
and so are they
and no one behind me reading over these things
no one behind me as I write this
but You

6

Ten years in the department of inhumanities
I taught myself self-torture
thesis splayed on a brick wall of words
while I grouted it in to structural support for
another brick and I'll finish
another brick and I'll finish
another brick and I'll finish

7

Burying the body backward
she conceived
she came

Time wants nothing more
than to imprison the thought

Flower boxes in his windows
eyelids in the night
gasp, as she came

the house a flying

8

I don't particularly
give a fuck about you Caesar.
I've no wish to please you.
I don't even care if
you're black or white.

Catullus, Carmen XCIII

9

You jump
your body follows
it lands
you land too

10

Since we met I've been throwing away clothes:
that dark blue German jacket, given me by Thalia
in exchange, like all beginning love;

that Guatemalan dream coat
Indian-made, and carrying something
of another world in its pockets

empty though they were; and then that
old shirt I threw away too, borrowed off a friend's back
in Moscow – he'd come to visit and I missed home.

Serpents shed their coats like lies,
the past being one of them.
You're the apple of all time, thought Adam

sharpening his hair. You join me.
We dine. Into the future. I don't need
these old ties, either. You join me.

Paolo and Francesca
reading together
the Book of Hours
fell to love

Her hand touching his
to turn the page
I'll be your page
said he

Stay your hand and feel
the hours that bound them apart
unfold in
to a volume of sighs
so quickened their passion
so out of breath

Be my Paolo, sweet reader
don't turn the page
stay my Francesca